The Chair

Written by Staci J Allen

Illustrated by
Alexandria Mesz

ISBN: 978-1-09836-532-5 (print)
ISBN: 978-1-09836-533-2 (eBook)

Dedicated to my sisters Lori and Tina – may sweet chair memories be a source of happiness always!

And to my mom, who spent hours making dad's chair extra cozy by crocheting afghan slip-covers!

He holds his new daughter in his arms.
He's unsure what to do with her. This feels
awkward. He's never held a baby before. Cautiously
he sits in the new chair. It feels awkward, too.
Stiff. New material. Never before sat in.
His arms are stiff as well as he cradles this new life.
She's forgiving, though, as she gazes into his eyes.
The chair is forgiving too as it welcomes this new
dad. He feels his body begin to relax as he settles
into the new chair with his baby daughter.
Slowly he begins to rock her – back and forth.
A new life begins.

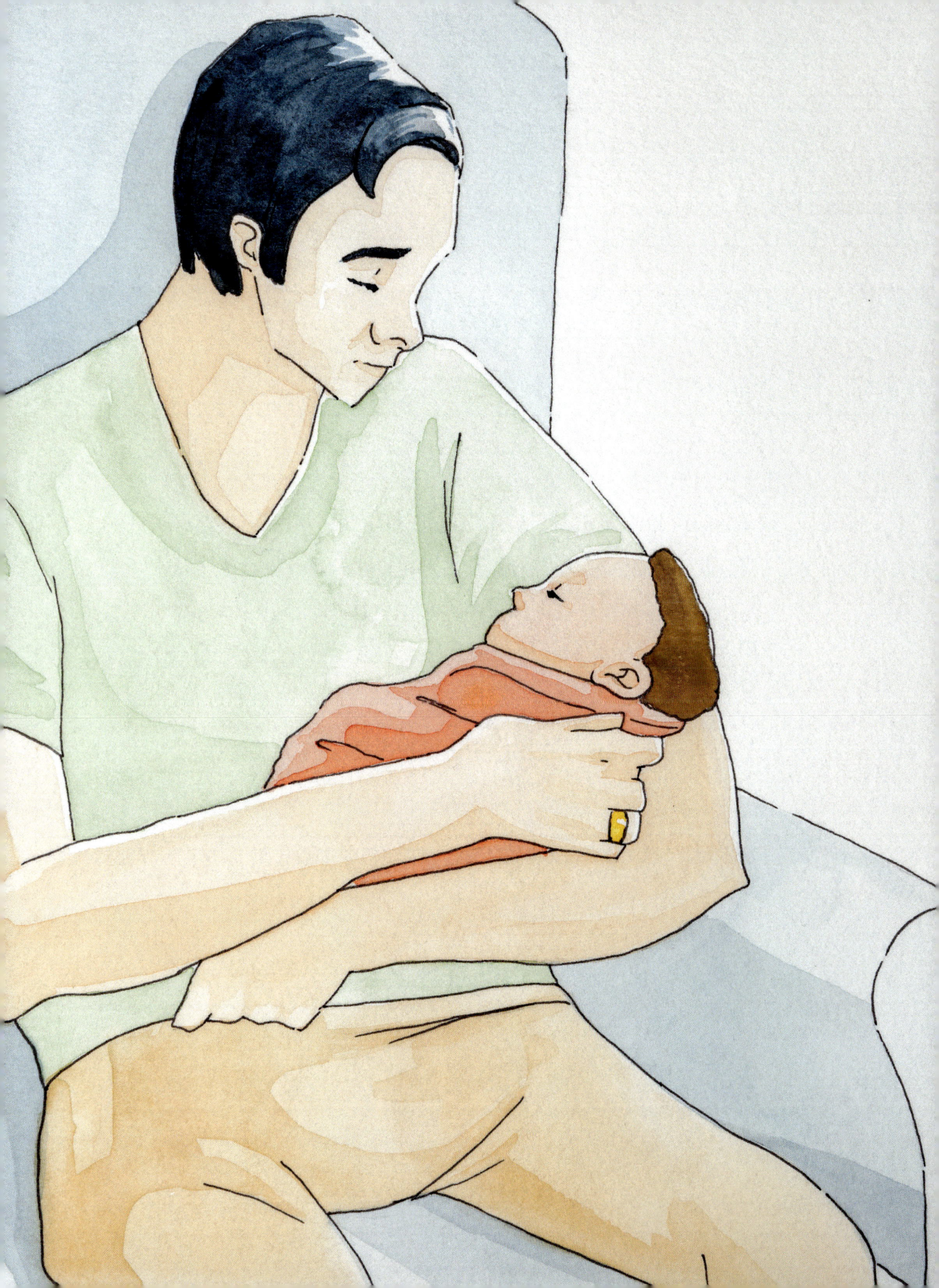

He sits in his chair with his leg tucked underneath him and his three young daughters cuddled in his arms. Safe in their daddy's arms, the toddlers melt into him. Safe in the comfort of his chair, he holds them close. Together they rock – back and forth. Daddy and his girls.

The chair sits empty but not for long. Three young girls race to see who gets to sit in dad's chair. The winner claims the chair as she throws herself into the rocker. She is victorious – this time. Her victory is short-lived though as he enters the room. The game is over. No words need to be said. Dad claims his rightful spot as he settles into his chair and slowly rocks back and forth. Dad's chair.

Night time arrives and the young girls prepare
for bed. His cheeks have been scrubbed clean and
he smells of aftershave. Leaning over the arm of
the chair, each daughter plants a sweet kiss on his
cheek. The day comes to an end with him sitting
in his chair – rocking back and forth.
Good-night, sleep tight.

She kneels next to his chair and leans in close with a look of determination, as homework is tackled. He sits in his chair with her math book in his lap, studying the assignment. The curtains have been pulled shut for the day and the lamp casts a soft glow as dad and daughter work together in solving math problems. With a father's explanation, the problem is understood. He hands the book back to her as she continues with her homework. He resumes watching his evening TV program – rocking back and forth in his chair. Problem solved.

Her heart has been broken. He knows how to fix everything but a broken teenage heart. He rocks in his chair, silently acknowledging her sadness. She is comforted by his presence and the sound of his chair. He rocks back and forth, wishing he could do anything to mend her broken heart. Teenage moments are challenging. A father's love is comforting. Tomorrow is a new day.

Gift-giving on Christmas mornings; televised football games and wrestling matches, westerns and mysteries; father-daughter conversations – both good and not so good – college plans, military life, new baby announcements; marriage proposals. Life takes place in the comfort of an overstuffed rocking chair, covered with a crocheted afghan. And still, he rocks back and forth.

He sits in his new chair in their new home as a new chapter of life begins. Once again, a colorful afghan has been lovingly crocheted for this new chair. This chair, meant for rocking grandbabies of all ages and stages; for welcoming adult children who return for weekend visits; for grandpa-chair races and giggles; for visiting and catching up with life. A new chair for a new stage of life. No longer the young man he used to be. He's older now and a little more tired. His days are filled with retirement things like reading his favorite westerns (over and over again), watching his favorite shows (over and over again), and squeezing in a nap or two following an afternoon of fishing and coffee with friends. His evenings are spent in companionship with his beloved. He rocks back and forth.

An empty chair sits in a quiet room while the
sound of a soothing cuckoo clock fills the silence.
Sadness is felt as hearts are broken.
No more rocking back and forth.
Time has stopped while grief takes over.

She sits in his chair, comforted by the feel of a cozy afghan and the lingering smells of his presence. Sweet memories flood her grieving heart. His arms have been replaced by the arms of his chair and she is comforted by the hug that comes as she sinks into the chair – rocking back and forth.

A different house, a different generation but yet the same chair. She holds her new grandson in her arms. She knows what to do as she has held babies before. She sits in the old chair. It feels comfortable. Overstuffed arms hold her close as she cradles this new life. He gazes into her eyes as she remembers. Slowly she begins to rock him – back and forth. A new life begins.

In memory of my dad who loved his cozy, afghan-covered chair but not as much as he loved his girls.

Feb 6, 1928 – April 2, 2012